It's another Quality Book from CGP

This book is for 11-14 year olds.

It contains lots of tricky questions designed
to make you sweat — because that's the only
way you'll get any better.

It's also got some daft bits in to try and make
the whole experience at least vaguely
entertaining for you.

What CGP is all about

Our sole aim here at CGP is to produce the highest quality
books — carefully written, immaculately presented and
dangerously close to being funny.

Then we work our socks off to get them out to you
— at the cheapest possible prices.

Contents

Statistics and Graphs

Angles & Other Bits

Algebra

Published by Coordination Group Publications Ltd.
Illustrated by Lex Ward and Ashley Tyson

Contributors:
Ruso Bradley
June Hall
Mark Haslam
Claire Thompson

ISBN: 978 1 84146 049 9

Groovy website: www.cgpbooks.co.uk
Printed by Elanders Hindson Ltd, Newcastle upon Tyne.
Clipart sources: CorelDRAW® and VECTOR.

1.1   *Questions on Big Numbers*

Always group your digits in threes (starting from the right) and split them up with a comma. If they've written them without commas, put your own in.

Q1 I have three cards, shown on the right. I can put these together so they make the number 196.

a) Use these numbers to make a number which is larger than 196.

....

b) Using the same numbers, make a number smaller than 196.

....

Q2 My mum is 61 years old, my dog, Alice, is 761 years old and my invisible friend Peter is 1,761 years old.

a) How do you write 61 in words?

....

b) Put my mum, Alice and Peter in order of age, starting with the youngest.

Youngest .... Oldest

Q3 Write the following numbers in words:

a) 102 ....

b) 3,570 ....

Q4 Write the following down as a number:

a) eight hundred and forty two   b) one thousand, five hundred and six.

....

1.2 *Questions on Plus and Minus*

no calculators!!

Q1 Do these questions as quickly as you can, without using your calculator:

a) 13 + 7 = 1 3
    _7_ +

c) 61 + 129 =

b) 23 + 39 = 2 3
    _3 9_ +

d) 1765 + 327 =

Q2 Do these questions as quickly as you can, still without using your calculator:

a) 24 - 5 = 2 4
    _5_ -

c) 873 - 289 =

b) 132 - 46 = 1 3 2
    _4 6_ -

d) 2948 - 1432 =

Q3 I have 2 bags of onion bhajis, one of which holds 42 bhajis. I empty them onto a plate, making 50 bhajis. How many bhajis were in the second bag?

....

Q4 After putting 50 onion bhajis on a plate, my clumsy friend drops them. I use 2 bags to throw them away. If one holds 8 bhajis, how many go in the other bag?

....

ALWAYS put the numbers in COLUMNS when you're adding... and check the UNITS, TENS & HUNDREDS line up.

1.3 *Questions on Times and Divide*

Q1 Do these questions as quickly as you can, without using your calculator:

a) 5 × 7 = ...

b) 12 × 10 = ...

c) 81 ÷ 9 = ...

d) 42 ÷ 7 = ...

Q2 Work out the following:

a) 70 × 7 = 7 0
        7 ×

b) 53 × 9 =

c) 117 ÷ 9 = 9⟌117

d) 246 ÷ 6 =

Q3 I have discovered the secret recipe for Froggatt's Lumpy Sprout Ketchup, which needs 342 mouldy sprouts to make 1 pot. I have decided to make 6 pots, to last me through the long cold winter. How many mouldy sprouts will I need ?

Q4 I have recently been sued by Froggatt's for selling 6 pots of Lumpy Sprout Ketchup for a total profit of 72p. I have been told I can only keep the profits on 1 pot, the rest going back to Mr Froggatt — how much money do I keep?

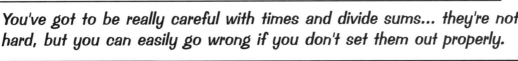

You've got to be really careful with times and divide sums... they're not hard, but you can easily go wrong if you don't set them out properly.

1.4 Questions on Times / Divide by 10, 100 etc

 <u>Multiplying / Dividing</u> by 10,100 or 1000 moves each digit 1, 2 or 3 places to the <u>left / right</u> — you just fill the rest of the space with zeros.

Q1 Carry out the following multiplications:

a) 51 × 10 = ...

b) 320 × 10 = ...

c) 14 × 100 = ...

d) 160 × 1000 = ...

e) 7.6 × 100 = ...

f) 5.487 × 10 = ...

Q2 Carry out the following divisions:

a) 350 ÷ 10 = ...

b) 1500 ÷ 100 = ...

c) 190,000 ÷ 1000 = ...

d) 20 ÷ 100 = ...

e) 1.6 ÷ 10 = ...

f) 410.36 ÷ 100 = ...

Q3 You have 8 jars of sweets, with the weights written on them.

a) Write down the letters of two jars, one of which contains 10 times the weight of the other.

....

b) Write down the letters of two jars, one of which contains 100 times the weight of the other.

....

Q4 If 100 rats cost £200, how much does 1 rat cost?

....

1.5   *Questions on Ordering Decimals*

Q1   Arrange the following decimals in order of size, largest first:
     3.4   3.04   4.03   1.607   0.0958   1.67

....

Q2   Arrange the following decimals in order of size, smallest first:
     10.5   1.05   15.9   3.789   9.801   0.99

....

Q3   Which is bigger, $30 \div 1000$ or $4 \div 100$?

     $30 \div 1000 =$ ....

     $4 \div 100 =$ ....

                    .... is the bigger number.

Q4   Which is smaller, 0.007×10 or 0.000007×1000?

     $0.007 \times 10 =$ ....

     $0.000007 \times 1000 =$ ....

                    .... is the smaller number.

Q5   The heights of 3 baby elephants are measured. John is found to be 1.2m high, Caroline measures 1.02m and Arthur is 0.95m. Who is the tallest?

....

Remember to look at the numbers before the decimal point first, then work right from the point to find the biggest numbers.

1.6   Questions on Multiples, Primes, Factors

The multiples of a number are just its times table.
Factors multiply together to make other numbers.

Q1   List all the multiples of 5 up to 60.

....

Q2   Find all the factors of 8.

....

Q3   List all the factors of 20 and 35.

....

....

a) Which numbers are in both lists?

....

b) Using your answer to part a), which is the
highest factor of both numbers?

....

Q4   List all the multiples of 6 and 9 up to 36.

....

....

What is the lowest number in both lists? ....

Q5   Find all the prime numbers between 1 and 10.

....

1.6 Questions on Multiples, Primes, Factors

Q6 Work out whether each of the following numbers is prime. (Answer Y/N.)

a) 42 ....

(Y/N) ....

b) 35 ....

(Y/N) ....

c) 41 ....

(Y/N) ....

d) 13 ....

(Y/N) ....

e) 69 ....

(Y/N) ....

f) 29 ....

(Y/N) ....

Q7 List all the multiples of 3 which are less than 50.

....

....

Is 45 a prime number? (Y/N) ....

_A prime number doesn't divide by anything, except itself and one —
so if you can find a number that divides exactly into it... it's not a prime._

1.7 Questions on Odd, Even, Square, Cube

 EVEN SQUARE ODD CUBE

Q1 List all the even numbers between 20 and 40.

....

Q2 List all the odd numbers between 30 and 50.

....

Q3 Find the first 6 square numbers.

$1 \times 1 =$ .... , $2 \times 2 =$ .... , ... ,

.... ' .... ' ....

Q4 Find the first 6 cube numbers.

$1 \times 1 \times 1 =$ .... , $2 \times 2 \times 2 =$ .... , ... ,

.... ' .... ' ....

Q5 From this list of numbers:

36   100   71   62   343   121

a) write down all the even numbers .... ,

b) write down all the odd numbers .... ,

c) write down all the square numbers .... ,

d) write down all the cube numbers ....

Learn the <u>first 10</u> of these numbers — you'll need them <u>at your</u> <u>fingertips</u>, so you can spot them a mile off in the Exam.

1.8 Questions on Ratios

Remember the Golden Rule: <u>Divide for One, then Times for All</u>.

Q1 If 7 caterpillars cost £1.40, how much will 2 caterpillars cost?

£ 1.40 = ... pence

1 caterpillar costs .... ÷ 7 = ... pence

2 caterpillars cost .... × 2 = ... pence.

Q2 Divide 700g of haggis in the ratio 3 : 4.

....

....

....

Q3 I have some friends coming round for dinner and want to cook my favourite fish pie. My recipe serves 4 people, but I will need enough pie for 9 people.

a) How many potatoes will I need to cook my fish pie for everyone?

....

b) How much haddock will I need?

....

RECIPE FOR MY
FAVOURITE FISH PIE

400 g haddock
8 large potatoes
1 tin mushy peas
12 eggs
1 pinch of salt
2 tb/spoons curry powder

c) If eggs come in boxes of 6, how many boxes should I buy?

....

....

....

1.9   *Questions on Money*

 If you've got pence and £ in the same question, make sure you put the pence in the right column — that's <u>after</u> the decimal point.

Q1   Work out the following additions:

a) £5.68 + £3.11 = £ 5.68
<u>£ 3.11</u> +

b) £2.50 + 89p =

Q2   Do the following subtractions:

a) £9.98 - £5.40 = £ 9.98
<u>£ 5.40</u> -

b) £17.10 - 99p =

Q3   Multiply the following:

a) £7.99 × 3 = £ 7.99
<u>   3</u> ×

b) £29.50 × 7 =

Q4   Divide the following:

a) £3.40 ÷ 5 = 5⟌3.40

b) £32.62 ÷ 2 =

Q5   If I can buy one red hot chilli pepper for 21p, how much will 9 cost?

....

Q6   If I can buy 6 CD's for £51, how much does each CD cost?

....

1.10 Questions on The Best Buy

*Don't just guess at this, 'cos it's dead easy to do it right —
divide by the price, then compare the amount you get per penny.*

Q1 Which is better value, 20 false nails for £3.99,
or 10 false nails for £2.99?

....

....

....

Q2 I can either buy 6 m of ribbon for £2.50, or 7 m of ribbon for £2.60.
Which is the better buy?

....

....

....

Q3 My local bakery is doing a special batch of olive bread,
which will be sold in three different sized loaves.

400 g
90p

800 g
£1-20

600 g
£1-00

a) Which is the best value loaf?

....

....

b) If I buy the best value loaf, how much change will I get from a £2 coin?

....

1.11 Questions on Long Multiplication

Remember — *put a zero under the units when you multiply by the extra number in the tens column.*

Q1 Jamie's Expensive Apple Mart sells apples by the dozen, and he charges £1.35 per apple. How much does Jamie charge for a dozen (12) apples?

£ 1.35
    12 ×
    ‾‾‾‾

‾‾‾‾‾
‾‾‾‾‾

Q2 At Johnnie's Cheap and Nasty Cheese Mart you can get 639 g of cheese for £1. How much cheese would you get for £35?

Q3 I have 37 boxes of coloured pencils.

a) If there are 67 pencils in each box, how many pencils are there altogether?

b) If there are 11 blue pencils in each box, how many blue pencils are there in total?

1.12   *Questions on Long Division*

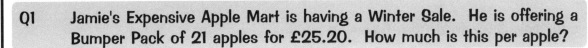

It's a good idea to write down the <u>first bit</u> of the <u>times table</u> for the number you're dividing by — it'll be easier to see what's going on.

Q1   Jamie's Expensive Apple Mart is having a Winter Sale. He is offering a Bumper Pack of 21 apples for £25.20. How much is this per apple?

$$21\,\overline{)\,25.20}$$

$$1 \times 21 = 21,$$
$$2 \times 21 = 42,$$
$$3 \times 21 = 63.$$

Q2   Johnnie has decided to make some more expensive cheese to sell at his mart. It now costs £13 for 663 g. How much cheese is this per £1?

Q3   A window cleaner needs to earn £300 per week to make a profit. If he charges £15 per window, how many windows does he need to clean each week?

Q4   After an all night Astronomy and Rockets Society Event, the organisers decide to put on buses to take home the 540 sleepy astronomers.

a) If each bus can take 30 astronomers, how many buses will be needed?

b) If they use double decker buses, which hold 45 people, how many will they need?

1.13 Questions on Calculators and BODMAS

Never underestimate the power of BODMAS... if you don't know how to use it, LEARN. It's easy to remember and you'll make mistakes without it.

Q1 Use your calculator to do the following sums:

a) 1972 + 475 = ...

b) 2040 - 67 = ...

c) 16 × 231 = ...

d) 588 ÷ 42= ....

Q2 Use the +/- button on your calculator to work out the value of:

a) -34 + 56 = ...

b) -43 - 12 = ...

c) 5 × -3 = ...

d) -7 × 6 = ...

Q3 Working out the part in brackets first, use your calculator to work out:

a) (3 + 2) × (6 - 4) = ...

b) (7 - 1) × (13 + 2) = ...

c) 8 ÷ (19 - 17) = ...

d) (6 + 9) ÷ (7 - 4)= ....

Q4 Work out the value of the following on your calculator, using the BODMAS rule to help you get things in the right order:

a) 6 + 4 × 6 = ...

b) 9 - 6 ÷ 3 = ...

c) 6 + 7 - 8 × 10 = ...

d) 1 + 4 ÷ 2 × 5 = ...

Q5 Use the BODMAS rule to work out the value of the following on your calculator:

a) $\dfrac{6 \times 4}{3 + 5}$ = ...

b) $\dfrac{7 \times 9}{5 - 2}$ = ...

c) $\dfrac{8 + 12}{14 - 4}$ = ...

d) $\dfrac{4 + 6}{12 \div 6}$ = ...

1.14 Questions on Using Formulas

Q1 The formula A = L × W is used to find the area of a rectangle.

a) Work out the value of the area, A, if L = 13 and W = 5.

$$A = L \times W$$

$$= 13 \times 5$$

$$= \text{..............}$$

b) Find the value of A when L = 26 and W = 4.

....

....

....

Q2 If y = 3(m + 3),

a) find the value of y when m = 2,

$$y = 3(m + 3)$$

$$y = 3(2+3)$$

$$= 3 (5)$$

$$= 3 \times 5 = \text{..............}$$

b) find the value of y when m = 4.

....

....

....

....

Q3 If p = q(r + s), find the value of p when q = 2, r = 6 and s = 1.

....

....

....

....

Remember — ALWAYS follow the *three steps*. *1) Write the formula, 2) write it again with the numbers, 3) work it out bit by bit.*

2.1 Questions on Perimeters

Always use the BIG BLOB METHOD to work out perimeter questions — that way you won't miss any of the sides... which means you'll <u>get it right</u>.

Q1 Work out the perimeter of the square and the equilateral triangle.

a)

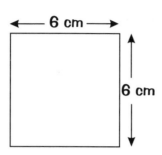

.............cm

b)

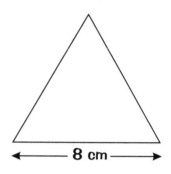

..............cm

Q2 Doris has cut out a piece of paper with some scissors. Work out the perimeter of the shape.

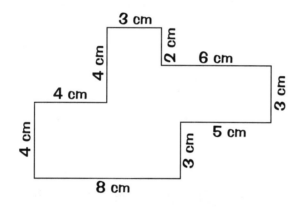

....

Q3 What is the perimeter of the parallelogram?

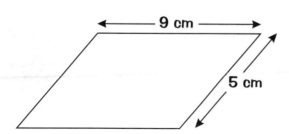

....

2.2 Questions on Areas

*Make sure you know these 2 area formulas inside out —
you'll be completely stuck without them, believe me...*

Q1 **What is the area of this rectangle?**

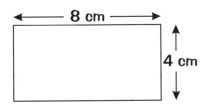

....cm^2

Q2 a) Write down the formula for the area of a triangle.

Area of a triangle = ...

b) Use your formula to work out the areas of the following triangles.

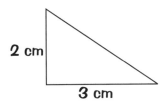

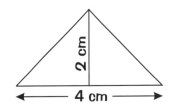

i) ....cm^2

ii) ....cm^2

Q3   **The area of a rectangular mouse mat is 500 cm^2, the width
of the mat is as shown. Calculate the length of the mat.**

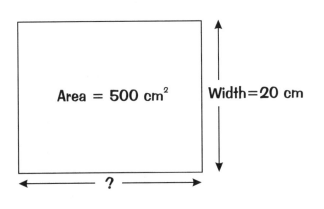

....cm

2.3   *Questions on Circles*

Remember which is which... the biggest problem with circles is that everyone gets the 2 formulas mixed up — that's half the battle really. Then you've just got to remind yourself that π is only a number and isn't at all scary.

Q1 **a)** Write down the formula for the circumference of a circle.

      Circumference of a circle = ...

      a) Write down the formula for the area of a circle.

      Area of a circle = ...

Q2   Taking π=3.14, calculate the circumference and the area of the circle below.

      a) Circumference = ...cm

      b) Area = ...cm²

(circle with diameter labelled 4 cm)

Q3   How many turns must a bicycle wheel of radius 0.5 m make to travel a distance of 100 m?

      ....

      ....

      ....

                                              Number of turns = ...

Q4   Gordon has invented a new pizza topping — Pepperoni and Digestive Biscuit. The recipe states that a third of the pizza should be covered with cheese.

      a) The radius of the pizza is **22 cm**, what is its area? ....

      ....

      b) What area of the pizza's surface should be covered with cheese?...........................

      ....

2.4 Questions on Solids and Nets

There are 4 nets you'll need to know really well — *TRIANGULAR PRISM, CUBE, CUBOID* and *PYRAMID*. They'll expect you to work out the areas, too.

Q1 Which of the two nets could be folded to form a cube?

a)

b)

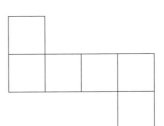

....

Q2 Draw a net of a triangular prism.

Q3 Below is the net of a triangular pyramid with a solid base.

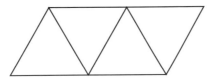

a) The area of each triangle is 1 cm².
What is the surface area of the resulting solid?.................................cm²

b) Draw a different net from the one
above that would also fold to make a
triangular pyramid with a solid base.

2.5   Questions on Volume and Capacity

This type is definitely the easiest — you just count up the little cubes.

Q1   The shapes below have been made from centimetre cubes. How many cubes are there in each shape?

a)

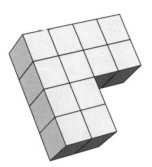

Number of cubes = ...

b)

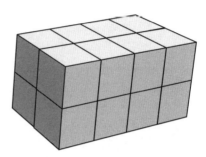

Number of cubes = ...

c)

Number of cubes = ...

d)

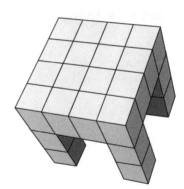

Number of cubes = ...

Q2   The shapes below have been made from centimetre cubes. The volume of a centimetre cube is 1 cubic cm. What is the volume of each shape in cubic cm?

a)

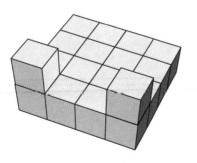

Volume = ... cm³

b)

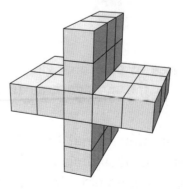

Volume = ... cm³

2.5 Questions on Volume and Capacity

Q3   What is the formula that connects the length,
width and height of a cuboid to its volume?

Volume of a cuboid = ...

Q4   Work out the volume of this box of Crunch Flakes.

....

....

Volume = ...

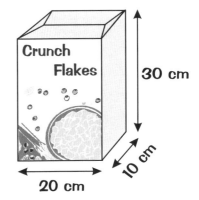

Crunch
Flakes

30 cm

20 cm

10 cm

Q5   What is the volume of a cube of side:

a) 1 cm

....

Volume of 1 cm cube = ...cm³

b) 2 cm

....

Volume of 2 cm cube = ...cm³

c) 3 cm

....

Volume of 3 cm cube = ...cm³

Q6   A box measures 5 cm by 4 cm by 2 cm.

a) What is the volume of the box?   ....

Volume of box = ...cm³

b) What is the volume of a box twice as
tall, twice as wide and twice as long?   ....

Volume of box = ...cm³

*Ok, so they've got a bit more tricky — but all you really need to do is...
(wait for it)... LEARN THE FORMULAS. Gosh, how did you guess...*

22

2.6 Questions on Symmetry

There's a line of symmetry if you can fold both sides exactly together. Have a go using <u>tracing paper</u> — it's easier to see (and you won't crease your book).

Q1 These shapes have only one line of symmetry. Draw the line of symmetry using a dotted line.

a)
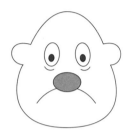

b)

c)
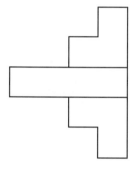

d)
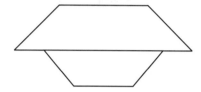

Q2 These shapes have more than one line of symmetry. Draw the lines of symmetry using a dotted line.

a)

b)
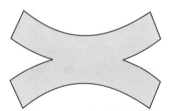

c)

d)
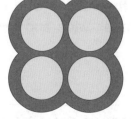

2.6 Questions on Symmetry

Q3 Find the order of rotational symmetry for these shapes.

a)

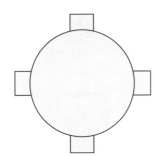

....

b)

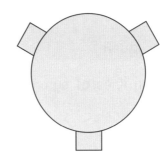

....

c)

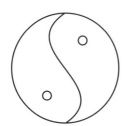

....

d)

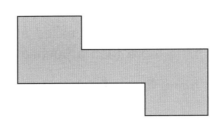

....

Q4 What is the order of rotational symmetry of the following capital letters?

a) b) c) d)

N   B   O   S

....

Q5 Tick the box if the plane is a plane of symmetry.

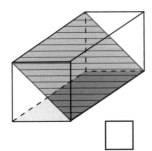 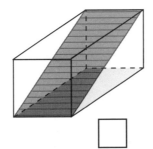 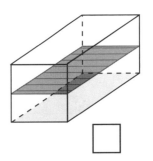

☐   ☐   ☐

You can work out the order of rotational symmetry by sticking your pen in the middle of the shape and spinning your book round — see how many times the shape looks the same before the book's back the right way up.

2.7 Questions on Shapes You Need To Know

Shape questions are <u>easy marks</u> — so make sure you know all about them... that means the symmetries and <u>everything</u>.

Q1 This is a square.

a) How many lines of symmetry does it have?

....

b) What is its order of rotational symmetry?

....

Q2 This diamond shape is called a rhombus. It is nothing more than a pushed over square.

a) How many lines of symmetry does it have?

....

b) What is its order of rotational symmetry?

....

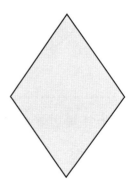

Q3 A parallelogram has two pairs of parallel sides. It is really just a pushed over rectangle.

a) How many lines of symmetry does it have?

....

b) What is its order of rotational symmetry?

....

Q4 Complete this drawing of a kite.

2.7 Questions on Shapes You Need To Know

Q5 An equilateral triangle has **3** sides of equal length.

a) How many lines of symmetry does it have?

....

b) What is its order of rotational symmetry?

....

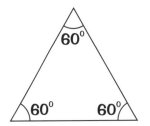

Q5 Put a name to each of these solids.

a)

....

b)

....

c)

....

d)

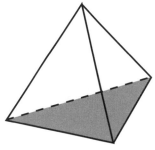

....

e)

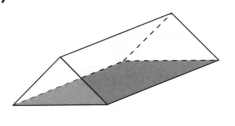

....

f)

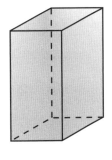

....

Name that shape... they're really keen on putting these in the Exam — gonna have to get learning those shape names, I reckon...

2.8   *Questions on Regular Polygons*

A polygon is a shape with lots of sides. Regular just means all the sides are the same length and all the angles are the same. So a regular polygon is...

Q1   Name these regular shapes.

a)

b)

c)
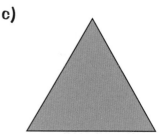

....

....

....

d)

e)

f)
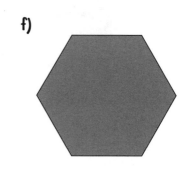

....

....

....

Q2   For each part of Q1 write down the number of lines of symmetry and the order of rotational symmetry.

a) Lines of symmetry = ...,   Order of rotational symmetry = ...
b) Lines of symmetry = ...,   Order of rotational symmetry = ...
c) Lines of symmetry = ...,   Order of rotational symmetry = ...
d) Lines of symmetry = ...,   Order of rotational symmetry = ...
e) Lines of symmetry = ...,   Order of rotational symmetry = ...
f) Lines of symmetry = ...,   Order of rotational symmetry = ...

Q3   Tick the box if the shape is regular.

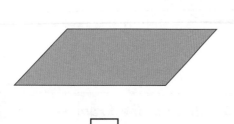

☐   ☐   ☐

2.8   Questions on Regular Polygons

Q4 a) Write down the formula for the exterior angle of a regular polygon.

Exterior angle = ...

b) Write down the formula for the interior angle of a regular polygon.

Interior angle = ...

Q5 a) Calculate the exterior angle of a hexagon.

....

b) Calculate the interior angle of a hexagon.

....

Q6   Calculate the missing angle in each of the following diagrams.

a)

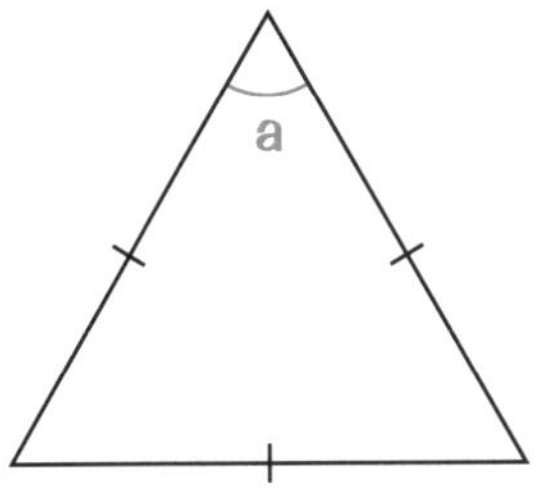

....
....

b)

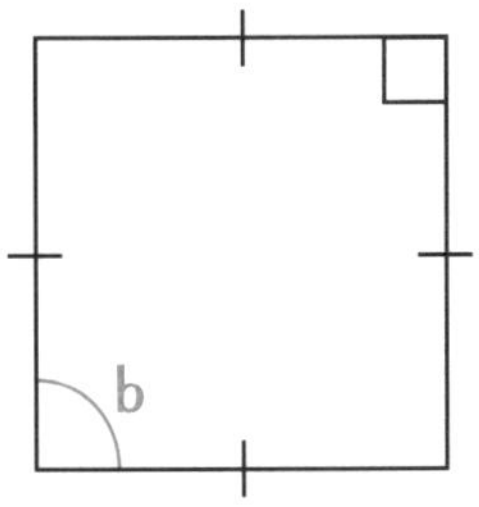

....
....

c)

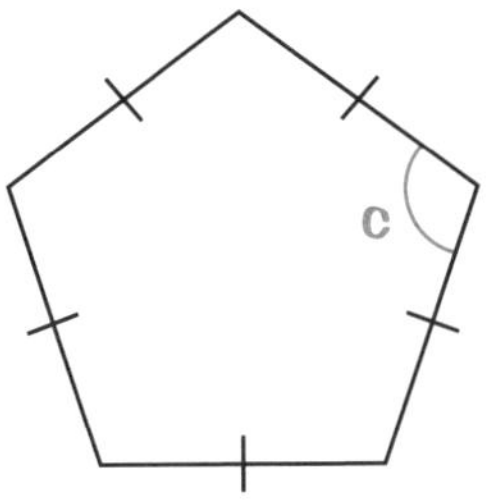

....
....

d)

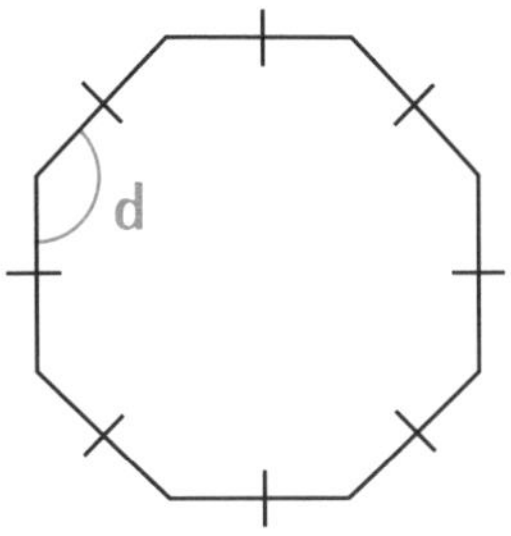

....
....

Here's a couple of matching formulas to engrave upon your memory... and REMEMBER — EXTERIOR ANGLE first, then <u>work out</u> the INTERIOR ANGLE.

3.1 Questions on Rounding Off

You always round off to the NEAREST NUMBER. It's a bit more tricky if it's exactly 1/2 WAY between 2 numbers — but then you just round UP.

Q1 Measure the length of the juggling alien to the nearest metre.

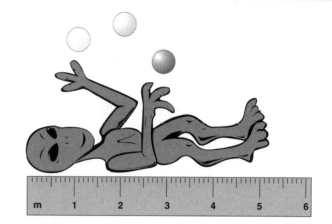

Height = ...m

Q2 Round the following to the nearest whole number:

a) 3.8 ....   d) 5.93 ....

b) 4.6 ....   e) 1.34 ....

c) 14.3 ....   f) 0.72 ....

Q3 Round these numbers to the nearest 10:

a) 12 ....   d) 44 ....

b) 23 ....   e) 128 ....

c) 61 ....   f) 65 ....

Q4 Round these numbers to the nearest 100:

a) 112 ....   d) 443 ....

b) 235 ....   e) 1285 ....

c) 616 ....   f) 653 ....

3.1 Questions on Rounding Off

Q5 Give these amounts to the nearest pound:

a) £1.12 ....   d) £24.20 ....

b) £4.25 ....   e) £5.50 ....

c) £14.51 ....   f) £0.57 ....

Q6 Give these weights to the nearest kilogram:

a) 4.35 kg ....   d) 10.45 kg ....

b) 1.65 kg ....   e) 35.46 kg ....

c) 0.67 kg ....   f) 1.97 kg ....

Q7 Nutmeg United have just played 4 games within the space of a week. Below are the crowd sizes for each match. Round each figure to the nearest 1000.

a) 13,456 ....

b) 21,822 ....

c) 16,737 ....

d) 9,742 ....

Q8 Round these decimals to the nearest tenth:

a) 0.34 ....   d) 1.34 ....

b) 0.67 ....   e) 2.84 ....

c) 0.23 ....   f) 45.98 ....

If you round up a 9, you've got to put a 0 in its place, even if it's after the decimal point... in other words, 1.97 to 1 dp would be 2.0, not just 2 on its own.

3.2   Questions on Estimating

Estimating is great — it means <u>less work</u>, which is nice. Instead of worrying about awkward numbers, you just put in easy ones instead...

Q1   **Estimate the answers to these questions.**

For Example: 19 × 11 ≈ 20 × 10 = 200.

a) 18 × 9 ≈ .... × .... = ...

b) 29 × 11 ≈ .... × .... = ...

c) 19 × 21 ≈ .... × .... = ...

d) 21 ÷ 9 ≈ .... ÷ .... = ...

e) 97 ÷ 9 ≈ .... ÷ .... = ...

f) 49 ÷ 11 ≈ .... ÷ .... = ...

Q2   **The ranger is almost 2 m tall.**
Estimate the height of the two birds.

a) Height of the small bird = ...m

b) Height of the large bird = ...m

3.3 Questions on Conversion Graphs

Q1 This graph shows the exchange rate between Euros (€) and Hong Kong dollars (HKD). How many HKD would you get for:

a) 5€ ....

b) 2€ ....

c) 8€ ....

How many Euros would you get for:

d) 80 HKD ....

e) 30 HKD ....

f) 55 HKD ....

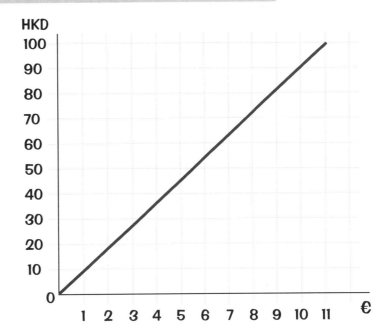

Q2 To hire a certain landscape gardener you need to pay according to the graph.

How much does it cost to hire the gardener for:

a) 1 hour ....

b) 3 hours ....

c) 5 hours ....

d) 1 ½ hours ....

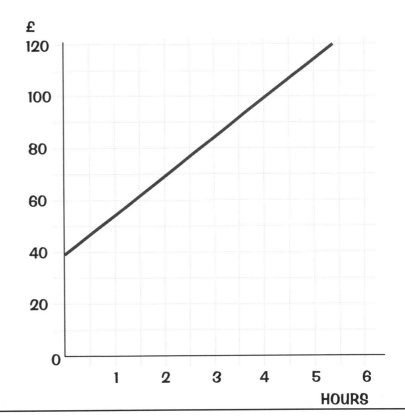

Remember, conversion graphs can be read 2 ways — you can convert from one thing to the other and back again.

3.4 Questions on Conversion Factors

SOME USEFUL METRIC CONVERSIONS	
10 mm = 1 cm	1000 mg = 1 g
100 cm = 1 m	1000 g = 1 kg
1000 m = 1 km	1000 ml = 1 l

Q1   Express each quantity in terms of the unit given in the brackets:

a) 4.5 m (cm) ....

d) 7.3 g (mg) ....

b) 3000 m (km) ....

e) 3.5 kg (g) ....

c) 3.2 km (m) ....

f) 50 kg (g) ....

Q2   Neil's Earth Membership Card states his height as **2.92** m.

a) What is his height in centimetres? ....cm

The card also states that his weight is 143 kg.

b) What is Neil's weight in grams? ....g

Q3   A large jug can hold 4 litres of liquid.

a) How many millilitres is this? ....ml

The jug is only a quarter full.

b) How many litres are of liquid are in the jug? l

c) How many millilitres is this? ....ml

Don't forget to <u>multiply</u> AND <u>divide</u> by the conversion factor... then see which is the sensible answer.

3.5 Questions on Metric and Imperial

IMPERIAL CONVERSIONS

1 foot = 12 inches
1 yard = 3 feet
1 gallon = 8 pints
1 stone = 14 pounds
1 pound = 16 ounces

APPROXIMATE CONVERSIONS

1 kg = 2.2 lbs
1 yard = 0.9 m
1 litre = 1.75 pints
1 in = 2.5 cm

1 gallon = 4.5 L
1 foot = 30 cm
1 metric tonne = 1 imperial ton
1 mile = 1.6 km

Q1 Express each quantity in terms of the unit given in the brackets:

a) 45 cm (inches) ....

b) 300 m (yards) ....

c) 3.2 km (miles) ....

d) 7.3 kg (pounds) ....

e) 3.5 kg (pounds) ....

f) 5.6 tonnes (tons) ....

Q2 Donald is on holiday in the USA. He sees a sign on the freeway stating that it is 120 miles to the Vail ski resort.

a) How far is this in kilometres? ....km

He turns on the radio to hear that 5 inches of snow fell overnight.

b) How many centimetres of snow is this? ....cm

Q3 Mr Gold's swimming pool can hold 50,000 litres of water.

a) How many pints of water is this? ....pt

b) How many gallons is this (to the nearest 1000 gallons)?

...................gallons

Q4 A sign on a low bridge states that only vehicles under 3.2 m tall can pass underneath.

Can a lorry 144 inches high pass under the bridge?

....

....

.... Yes/No

You've got to learn these conversions — go on, there aren't many of them...

3.6 Questions on Fractions

All you do is see how many equal parts you've got (the bottom number) and look for how many of them are shaded (the top number) — then cancel if you can...

Q1 What fraction of each of the following shapes is shaded?

a)

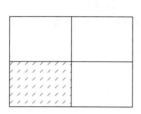

....

b)

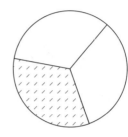

....

c)

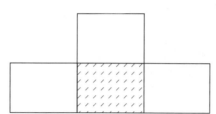

....

d)

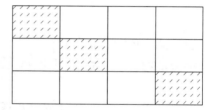

....

Q2 Shade each diagram to show the fraction.

a) $\frac{1}{4}$

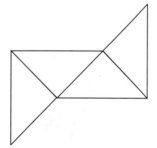

b) $\frac{2}{5}$

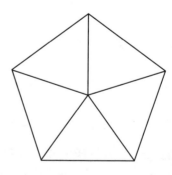

Q3 Which is bigger?

a) $\frac{1}{6}$ or $\frac{2}{13}$ ....

b) $\frac{3}{10}$ or $\frac{4}{13}$ ....

c) $\frac{12}{23}$ or $\frac{15}{28}$ ....

d) $\frac{1}{3}$ or $\frac{56}{158}$ ....

3.6   *Questions on Fractions*

Q4   Change these top-heavy fractions to mixed numbers.

a) $\dfrac{5}{2}$ = ...

b) $\dfrac{7}{3}$ = ...

c) $\dfrac{41}{10}$ = ...

d) $\dfrac{22}{5}$ = ...

Q5   Work out the following:

a) $\dfrac{1}{5} + \dfrac{3}{5}$ = ...

b) $\dfrac{1}{10} + \dfrac{4}{10}$ = ...

c) $\dfrac{4}{7} + \dfrac{5}{14}$ = ...

d) $\dfrac{3}{8} + \dfrac{3}{4}$ = ...

Q6   Calculate:

a) $\dfrac{1}{5} \times \dfrac{3}{5}$ = ...

b) $\dfrac{1}{10} \times \dfrac{4}{10}$ = ...

c) $\dfrac{4}{7} \times \dfrac{5}{6}$ = ...

d) $\dfrac{3}{8} \times \dfrac{3}{4}$ = ...

Q7   Calculate the following:

a) $\dfrac{1}{6}$ of £1.80 = ...

b) $\dfrac{3}{7}$ of 14 kg = ...

c) $\dfrac{5}{6}$ of 12 months = ...

When you get a "fraction of..." type question, just divide by the bottom and times by the top — what could be simpler..

3.7   Questions on Fractions, Decimals, %'s

Q1   Give the shaded area of these shapes as a fraction and a percentage of the whole.

a)
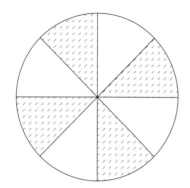

Percentage = ...

Fraction = ...

b)
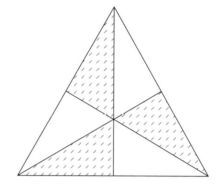

Percentage = ...

Fraction = ...

c)
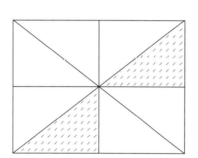

Percentage = ...

Fraction = ...

d)
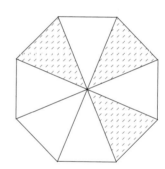

Percentage = ...

Fraction = ...

Q2   Change these fractions to percentages.

a) Fraction = $\frac{1}{2}$, percentage = ...

b) Fraction = $\frac{3}{4}$, percentage = ...

c) Fraction = $\frac{6}{10}$, percentage = ...

d) Fraction = $\frac{3}{5}$, percentage = ...

When you've got to go from fractions to percentages, ALWAYS go via decimals... it'll make life far easier.

3.7   Questions on Fractions, Decimals, %'s

Changing a percentage to a decimal just means moving the decimal point 2 places to the left. Piece of cake.

Q3   Change these percentages to decimals.

a) Percentage = 50%, decimal = ...

b) Percentage = 20%, decimal = ...

c) Percentage = 35%, decimal = ...

d) Percentage = 41%, decimal = ...

Q4   Match these cards into five sets that show the same number.

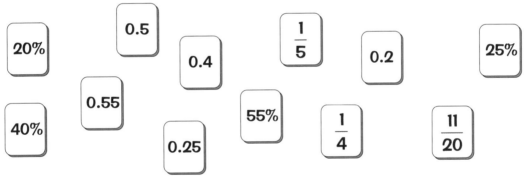

Set 1: .... = ... = ...

Set 2: .... = ... = ...

Set 3: .... = ... = ...

Set 4: .... = ... = ...

Set 5: .... = ... = ...

3.8 Questions on Percentages

To find "something % of something else" without your calculator, write the % as a decimal (by moving the point) then multiply by the "something else".

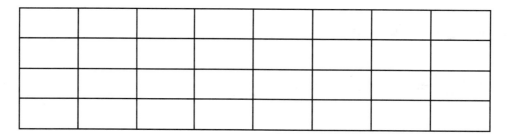

Q1 Shade $\frac{1}{4}$ of the diagram below:

What percentage of the diagram have you shaded? ....

Q2 Without a calculator work out:

a) 50% of £12 = ...

b) 25% of £12 = ...

c) 10% of 50 ml = ...

d) 20% of 125 kg = ...

no calculators!!

Q3 A social club has 500 members.

a) If 62% of members are male, what percentage are female? ....

b) If children are not allowed to be members, how many members of the club are men?

....

....

c) One night the great Johnny Vulcan was performing at the club. 80% of members turned out to see him sing. How many members was this?

....

....

d) How many members didn't turn out to see Johnny?

....

....

3.8   *Questions on Percentages*

Q4   There are 100 pupils at a school.

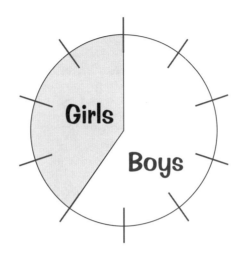

a) How many of the pupils at the school are boys?

....

b) How many of the pupils are girls?

....

c) What percentage of the pupils are boys?

....

Q5   Crimchester Police report a 14% increase in burglaries since last year, when 450 burglaries were recorded.

How many burglaries have there been this year?

....

....

Q6   In a sale a caravan was reduced by £110 from £990. What percentage reduction is this of the original price?

....

....

Only use the % button on your calculator when you're sure you know how it works — or things will just go pear-shaped.

4.1   Questions on Averages and Range

Remember the GOLDEN RULE — put things IN ORDER OF SIZE first... see, they're not too bad really.

Q1   Find the mode of this set of numbers: 4, 3, 6, 4, 4, 2, 3, 2

....

Q2   Find the median of this set of measurements:
12m, 16m, 17m, 16m, 13m, 18m, 15m, 16m

....

....

Q3   Below is a table of goals scored by members of
Millom Men's Netball Team during the previous season.

9	9	7	10	10	5
10	7	9	12	8	10

a) Find the median of this set of data.

....

b) What is the modal number of goals scored?

....

Q4   For 12 days, Dennis kept a record of how many minutes late
his train was, and recorded this data in the table below.

10	5	5	8	3	5
12	5	0	5	3	7

Find the modal average for these times.

....

4.1   Questions on Averages and Range

Remember — the MEAN is the one you have to *work out*.

Q5   Find the mean of this set of numbers: 2, 3, 4, 3, 6, 2, 3, 1

....

....

Q6   Find the range of this set of measurements:
100 cm, 120 cm, 99 cm, 121 cm, 103 cm, 107 cm, 98cm, 120 cm.

....

Q7   Kev decided to keep a record of the temperature, in °C, at 4 pm each day for 2 weeks during his summer holiday. His results were as follows:
20, 15, 14, 16, 17, 18, 23, 20, 13, 15, 17, 20, 23, 14

a) Find the mode of these temperatures.

....

b) Find the median.

....

c) What is the range of these temperatures?

....

d) What was the mean daily temperature at 4 pm during that 2 week period, in °C?

....

....

....

....

4.2 Questions on Frequency

Always do a tally to start with — it's really important you don't miss any of the bits out, or it'll muck your answers up good and proper.

Q1 Sian was reading a book about **UFO** sightings, and made a note of the number of times the words "strange light in the sky" appeared on each of the first 20 pages.

6; 21; 18; 10; 20; 13; 22; 12; 11; 5;
6; 14; 22; 15; 13; 16; 25; 11; 30; 29

a) Complete the tally and frequency rows of the chart below.

No of times	5	6	7	8	9	10	11	12	13	14	15	16	17	18	19	20	21	22	23	24	25	26	27	28	29	30
Tally																										
Frequency																										

b) How many pages had these words between 1 and 10 times? (Including 1 and 10)

....

c) How many pages contained this phrase between 21 and 30 times? (Inc. 21 & 30)

....

Q2 Paul did a survey on the teachers of his school, to see whether they could do his Maths homework. Their marks out of 30 are shown below.

29, 10, 28, 27, 11, 23, 14, 19, 17, 27, 29, 30, 25, 13, 21, 27,
14, 30, 20, 30, 19, 27, 7, 18, 27, 8, 18, 10, 25, 7, 19, 25

Complete this tally / frequency chart to show these results.

Marks	0 – 5	6 – 10	11 – 15	16 – 20	21 – 25	26 – 30
Tally						
Frequency						

4.2 Questions on Frequency

You just have to decide which group each measurement goes in, then do a tally, like before. Easy lemons...

Q3 Jane measured 20 hedgehogs that came into her garden over the holidays. The lengths are shown below:

10 cm, 9 cm, 15 cm, 23 cm, 13 cm, 17 cm, 12 cm,
8 cm, 17 cm, 19 cm, 23 cm, 22 cm, 20 cm, 16 cm,
18 cm, 13 cm, 24 cm, 8 cm, 19 cm, 6 cm.

a) Complete the tally and frequency rows in the chart below.

Hedgehogs seen (H)	0 < H ≤ 5	5 < H ≤ 10	10 < H ≤ 15	15 < H ≤ 20	20 < H ≤ 25
Tally					
Frequency					

b) Use the space below to draw a bar chart showing this information.

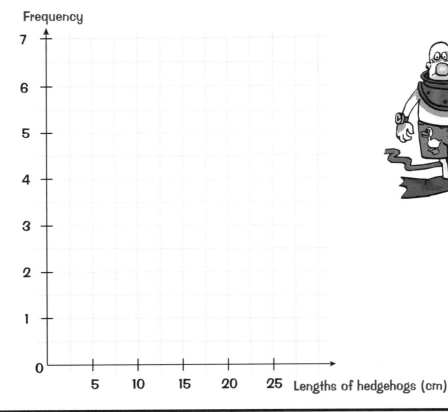

SECTION FOUR — STATISTICS AND GRAPHS

4.3 Questions on Graphs and Charts

You need to know all these different charts, so keep doing these 2 pages until you're happy with them.

Q1 Richard wanted to find out if feeding his tadpoles different types of food made them more likely to become frogs. He fed 1000 of them salad, 1000 bits of bacon, 1000 lamb chops and 1000 prime steak. His results were as follows:

	Salad	Bacon	Lamb	Steak
Frogs	100	1000	800	700

represents 200 tadpoles which turned into frogs. Use this to complete the pictogram shown below.

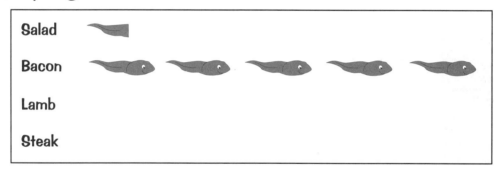

Salad

Bacon

Lamb

Steak

Q2 100 children were asked what their favourite colour was, each school year for 5 years. Numbers of those who chose purple are shown below.

1994	1995	1996	1997	1998
35	50	55	65	70

Plot these results on the graph below, then join the points up to form a line graph, or frequency polygon.

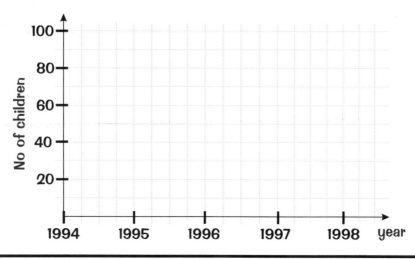

4.3 Questions on Graphs and Charts

Q3 Look at the two scatter graphs below, and state what the correlation is, if any.

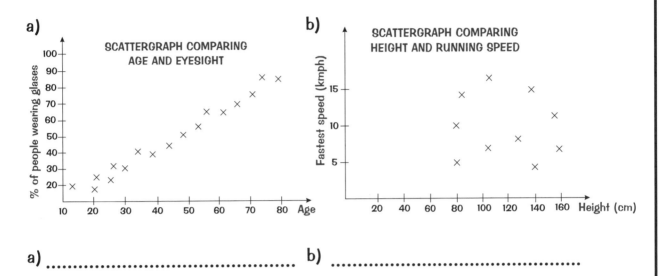

a) .... b) ....

Q4 In a recent survey, it was found that, out of 180 people questioned, 90 owned a dog, 20 owned a tarantula, 40 owned a cat and 30 owned no pets at all.

a) Complete the table below, to relate these numbers to angles in a pie chart.

Pet	Dog	Tarantula	Cat	No Pet
Number	90	20		
Angle	180°			

b) Use a protractor or angle measurer to construct a pie chart for this information.

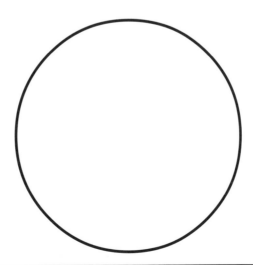

*Yeah, pie charts are a bit tricky, I admit, but the secret is to remember that the **TOTAL of EVERYTHING = 360°**. You've got to find that multiplier...*

4.4 Questions on Probability

Probability always has a value between 0 and 1 — if it's 0, the thing's DEFINITELY NOT going to happen... if it's 1, it DEFINITELY IS going to happen.

Q1 For each of the following events, say whether you think they are certain, likely, even, unlikely or impossible:

a) Monday will follow Sunday,

....

b) you will get a head when you toss an unbiased coin,

....

c) if your head is cut off, it will grow back in less than a week.

....

Q2 Put a letter on the probability scale below for each of the following events, to represent the probability of it happening. Explain your answers.

a) You will get wet if you jump into the sea.

Explanation ....

b) You will throw a dice and get a 6.

Explanation ....

c) If I drop my toast it will land butter side down.

Explanation ....

d) If I kiss a frog, it will turn into a handsome prince.

Explanation ....

```
0                                                    1
```

4.4   *Questions on Probability*

Q3   I have 6 football cards which I collected from teabags. I have 3 of Gazza, 2 of Ronaldo and 1 of David Beckham. My friend Gemma picks one at random.

a) What is the probability of Gemma picking Gazza?

....

b) What is the probability of her picking David Beckham?

....

Q4   In the National Lottery the balls are numbered 1 to 49 and are picked at random. What is the probability that the first number will be 10 or higher?

....

Q5   In my cupboard at home I have 8 identical bags. 1 contains tapes, 2 contain clothes and shoes, 4 contain books and 1 has got lots of money in it.

a) What is the probability of picking out the bag of money at random?

....

b) What is the probability of picking a bag which doesn't have any money in it?

....

Q6   List the 4 possible outcomes if I toss 2 coins together.

<u>1st go</u>   ....   <u>2nd go</u>   ....

            ....

            ....

            ....

What is the probability that I will get just 1 head?

....

Two heads are better than one... finding the probability of "just one head" is a bit tricky — you always forget that there are __2 ways__ of getting "just one head".

4.5   *Questions on Coordinates*

You've got to get your coordinates in the right order — or they're totally useless. *X always comes before Y...* quite easy to remember, isn't it.

Q1   Write down the coordinates of the points A, B, C and D.

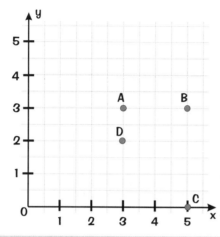

A ....

B ....

C ....

D ....

Q2   Plot the points E(1,1), F(3,1), G(4,3) and H(2,3) on the grid below.

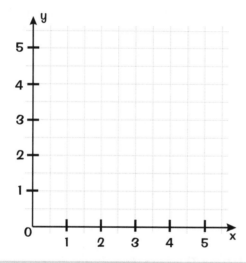

Q3   Plot the points J(4,2) and K(1,5) on the grid below. Add 2 more points, L and M, so that JKLM is a square. Write the coordinates of L and M below.

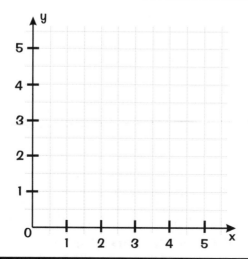

L   ....

M   ....

4.5   *Questions on Coordinates*

*It gets confusing when one coordinate is positive and one's negative —
your best defence is just to remember the order they're written in.*

Q4   Write down the coordinates of the points P, Q, R and S.

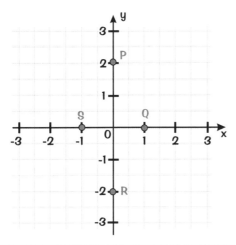

P ....

Q ....

R ....

S ....

Q5   Plot the points T(-1,1), U(-1,-3), V(3,-3) and W(3,1) on the grid below.

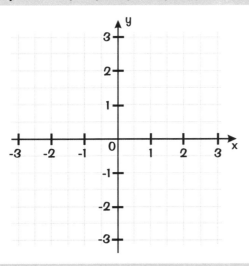

Q6   Plot the points X(-4,-2) and Y(2,-2) on the grid below. Add a point, Z, which is
halfway between X and Y, in a straight line. Write the coordinates of Z below.

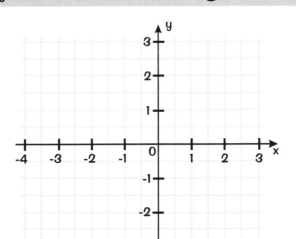

Z ....

4.6   *Questions on Line Graphs*

Learn what the 4 main graphs look like — <u>horizontal</u>, <u>vertical</u> and the main <u>diagonals</u>... they're not hard, but it's easy to get them mixed up with each other.

Q1   If the graph shown is the line x = 1, draw the line x = 2, on the same grid.

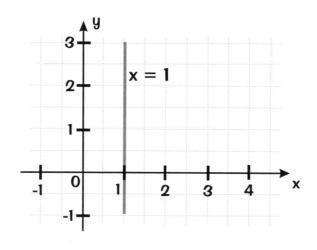

Q2   On the graph paper below, draw the following lines:

a) y = 3,

b) x = -1,

c) y = x.

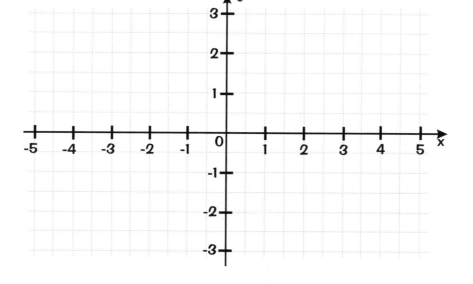

Q3   Complete this table of values using the equation y = x + 2.

x	-3	-2	-1	0	1	2	3
y	-1					4	5

4.6   *Questions on Line Graphs*

Make sure you know your coordinates stuff <u>before</u> you plot any points — or things'll go haywire. You'll either get a straight line or smooth curve, so double check any points that look wrong... they probably are.

Q4   Use the table of values from Q3 to plot the graph of y = x + 2.

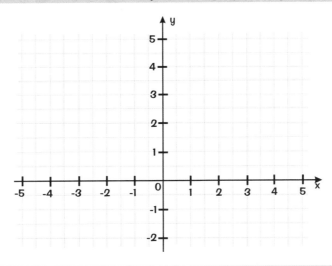

Q5   Complete the table of values below, using the equation y = x² - 6.

x	-3	-2	-1	0	1	2	3
x^2	9	4					9
y=x²-6	3	-2					3

a) Plot these points on the graph opposite.

b) Draw in the curve carefully (without using a ruler) and label it y = x² - 6.

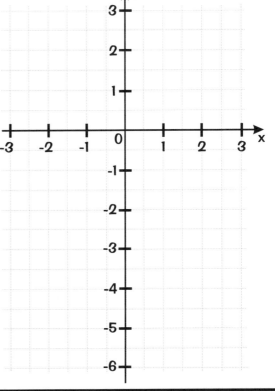

5.1 Questions on Clocks & Calenders

So you know what 24 hour clock is... well, it's about time...

The main thing to remember with time questions is the conversions between hours, minutes and seconds... 0.5 minutes is NOT 50 seconds...

 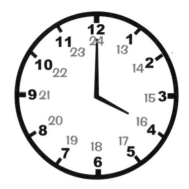

Q1 The times below are given using the 24 hour system. Using am or pm, give the equivalent time for a 12 hour clock:

a) 1000 ....

b) 1201 ....

c) 0001 ....

d) 1430 ....

e) 1720 ....

f) 2255 ....

Q2 The times below are taken from a 12 hour clock. Give the equivalent 24 hour readings:

a) 10.30 pm ....

b) 11.22 am ....

c) 12.30 am ....

d) 12.30 pm ....

e) 9.15 am ....

f) 3.33 pm ....

Q3 Convert the following into hours and minutes:

a) 3.5 hours ....

b) 1.25 hours ....

c) 5.2 hours ....

d) 3.75 hours ....

e) 2.3 hours ....

f) 1.7 hours ....

5.1 Questions on Clocks & Calenders

Q4 Convert the following into just hours:

a) 4 hours and 30 minutes ....

b) 1 hour and 6 minutes ....

c) 15 minutes ....

d) 5 hours 20 minutes ....

Q5 Clifford is taking the train from Hykeham to Tadley.

The train timetable shows what time trains leave Hykeham and arrive at Tadley.

TRAIN TIMETABLE: HYKEHAM TO TADLEY					
Depart Hykeham:	0915	1134	1345	1536	1658
Arrive Tadley:	1023	1234	1456	1649	1803

a) Clifford catches the train at 0915. What time does the train pull into Tadley station? ....

b) How long did the journey take? ....

c) Clifford's brother Martin is also travelling to Tadley and he catches the train at 1.45 pm. How long does his journey take? ....

Q6 The first day of January 1999 was a Friday.

a) On what day of the week did 7 January fall? ....

b) On what day of the week did 24 January fall? ....

c) How many days are there in January? ....

d) On what day of the week did 15 February fall? ....

Don't try and do it in your head — write down each step as you go. That way you'll pick up all those nice easy marks that it'd be a real shame to waste.

5.2 Questions on Bearings

Remember — you ALWAYS measure bearings as angles from the NORTH LINE...
if there isn't one drawn in, *do it yourself*.

Q1 Write down the three figure bearings of the following compass directions:

a) North ....

d) West ....

b) South ....

e) North-East ....

c) East ....

f) South-West ....

Q2 Measure the bearing of:

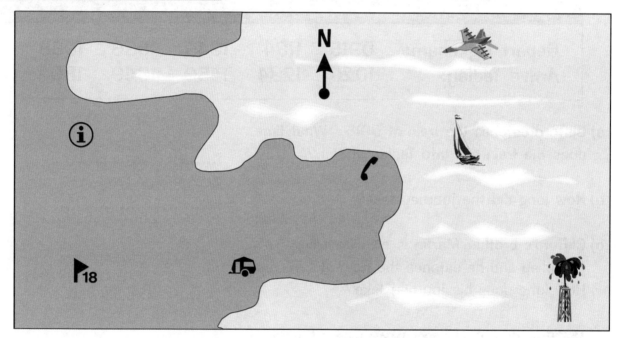

a) the golf course ⚑18 from the tourist information office ⓘ ....

b) the tourist information office ⓘ from the golf course ⚑18 ....

c) the caravan site ⌂ from the golf course ⚑18 ....

d) the golf course ⚑18 from the caravan site ⌂ ....

e) the phone box 📞 from the caravan site ⌂ ....

5.3   *Questions on Maps and Scales*

Q1   The scale on a map is "1 cm to 1 km". How many kilometres in real life are represented by:

a) 2 cm on the map ....

b) 4 cm on the map ....

c) 10 cm on the map ....

d) 5 cm on the map ....

e) 15 cm on the map ....

f) 100 cm on the map .... ?

Q2   The map below has a map with a scale "1 cm to 10 km".

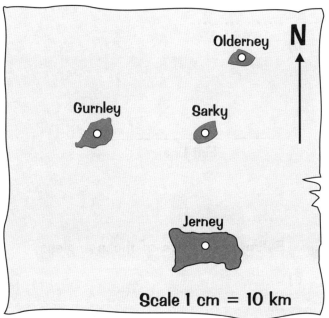

Scale 1 cm = 10 km

By first measuring the distance in centimetres on the map and then converting into kilometres, find:

a) the distance in real life from the centre of Jerney to the centre of Sarky

....

....

b) the distance in real life between the centre of Gurnley and the centre of Olderney

....

....

Remember — count the km along the cm marks on your ruler...

5.4   *Questions on Lines and Angles*

Make sure you can do Q1 before you go any further — once you know these 4 main angles, you'll find it a whole lot easier to estimate others.

Q1   The angles below are rather important. Write down the size of each of them.

a)

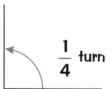

$\frac{1}{4}$ turn

....

b)

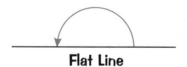

Flat Line

....

c)

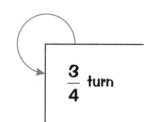

$\frac{3}{4}$ turn

....

d)

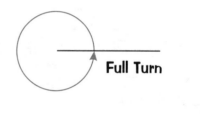

Full Turn

....

Q2   Estimate the size of these angles:

a)

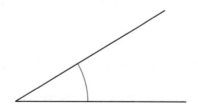

....

b)

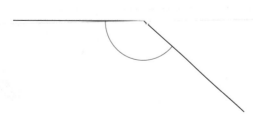

....

c)

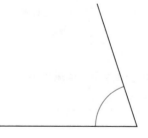

....

d)

....

5.5 Questions on Measuring Angles

Q1 Using either an angle measurer or a protractor measure the following angles:

a)

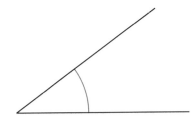

....

b)

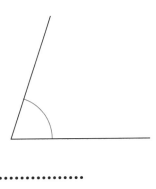

....

c)

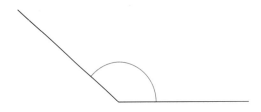

....

d)

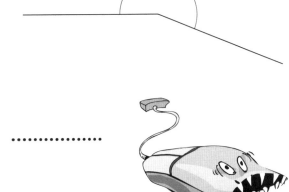

....

Q2 Using the line given as a base draw:

a) an example of an acute angle, clearly labelling the size of the angle

_____

b) an example of an obtuse angle, clearly labelling the size of the angle.

_____

Remember — protractors have two scales... one going one way and one the other. You've got to _measure from the 0^0_, not the 180^0.

SECTION FIVE — ANGLES & OTHER BITS

5.6   *Questions on Calculating Angles*

Nope, still haven't got rid of those darn angles... if you don't know those <u>5 important angle rules</u> yet, <u>get learning</u> — you're just about to need them.

Q1   **Work out the lettered angles:**

a)

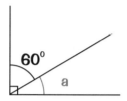

a = ...

c)

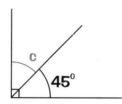

c = ...

b)

b = ...

d)

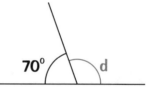

d = ...

Q2   **For each of the following work out the size of the angle marked x.**

a)

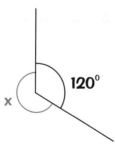

x = ...

c)

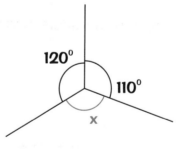

x = ...

b)

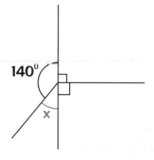

x = ...

d)

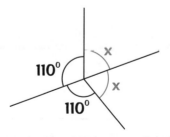

x = ...

5.6   *Questions on Calculating Angles*

Q3   Given that the angles inside a triangle always add up to 180°, work out the missing angles.

a)

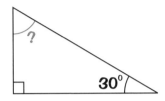

Missing angle = ...

c)

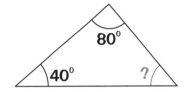

Missing angle = ...

b)

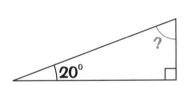

Missing angle = ...

d)

Missing angle = ...

Q4   Given that the angles inside a quadrilateral always add up to 360°, work out the missing angles.

a)

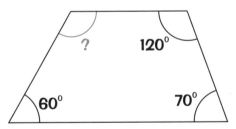

Missing angle = ...

c)

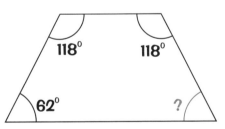

Missing angle = ...

b)

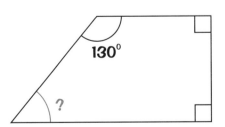

Missing angle = ...

d)

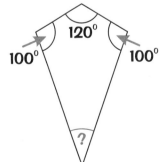

Missing angle = ...

The tricky bit is remembering the rules — then it's just all adding and subtracting.

SECTION FIVE — ANGLES & OTHER BITS

5.7 Questions on Three-Letter Angle Notation

Well, it's a bit of a mouthful, I admit — but believe me, it's not complicated. Basically, the <u>middle letter is the one where the angle is</u>. That's it, really.

Q1 This is a quadrilateral ABCD.

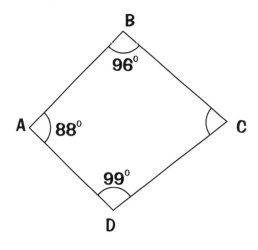

a) Write down the size of angle ABC ....

b) Write down the size of angle DAB ....

c) Write down the size of angle CDA ....

d) Work out the size of angle BCD ....

Q2 In a triangle XYZ, the angle XYZ = 90°, angle YXZ = 60° and angle XZY = 30°.

a) Draw a rough sketch of the triangle XYZ, clearly labelling X, Y and Z.

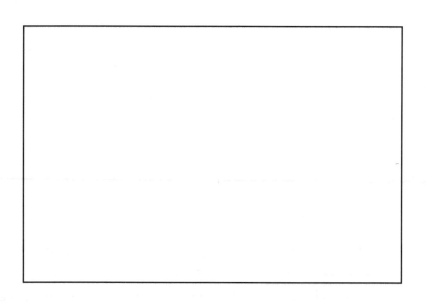

5.8 Questions on Congruence

How many of these shapes are congruent to the one in the box?

Number of congruent shapes = ...

Q2 Find the pairs of congruent shapes.

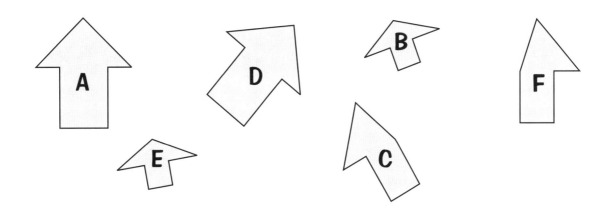

a) Shape .... is congruent to shape ....

b) Shape .... is congruent to shape ....

c) Shape .... is congruent to shape ....

Tracing paper's your best bet here... OK, you can usually guess which shapes look the same, but with tracing paper you can be sure they're exactly the same — and it's the easiest thing in the world.

5.9   *Questions on Reflection*

*Nothing fancy here, is there — reflection's just mirror drawing really.
And we've all done that before...*

Q1   Reflect each shape in the line x = 4.

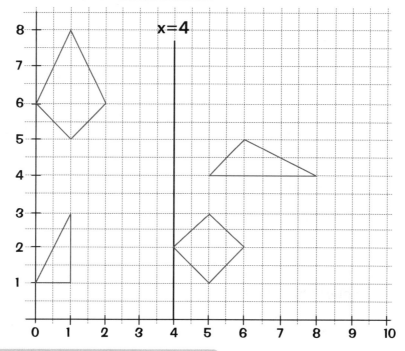

Q2   Reflect each shape in the line y = x.

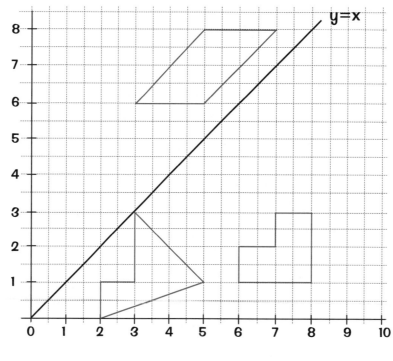

5.10   *Questions on Rotation*

Q1 The centre of rotation for each of these diagrams is **X**. Rotate each shape as asked then draw the new position of the shape onto each of the diagrams below.

a) 180° clockwise (or ½ turn).

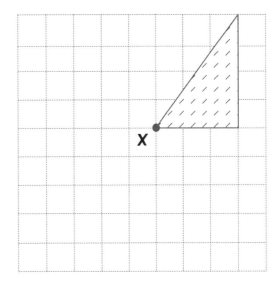

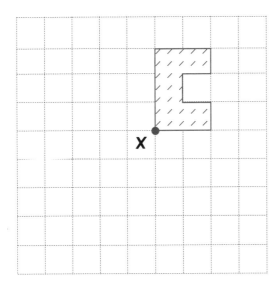

b) 90° clockwise (or ¼ turn clockwise).

c) 270° anticlockwise (or ¾ turn anticlockwise).

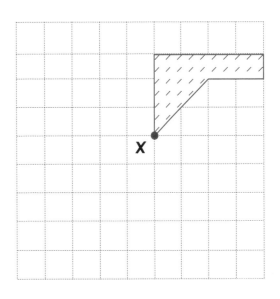

 A ½ turn clockwise is the same as a ½ turn anti-clockwise — and a ¼ turn clockwise is the same as a ¾ turn anti-clockwise. Great fun, innit...

6.1 Questions on Balancing

See — algebra ain't so bad after all. Just an alien on some scales... and there you were thinking it was all x's and y's...

Q1 The scales below are perfectly balanced.

a) How much does one alien weigh? ....

b) How many aliens would be needed on the right hand side of the scales below to make them balance?

....

c) There is a new breed of alien in town. They each weigh 10 kg. How many kilograms need to be placed on the left to balance the scales?

....

6.1 Questions on Balancing

Q2 Monsieur Blanc is renovating an old elephant. Currently it lays in pieces on his garage floor. Out of interest he places some of the more important bits on a set of balance scales:

2 Klump Couplings = 1 Forward Back Acter

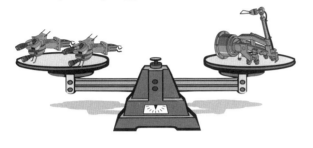

1 Nose Arm = 4 Klump Couplings

a) Work out what should go in the blank space.

i) How many klump couplings?

ii) How many forward back acters?

iii) How many nose arms?

iv) How many klump couplings?

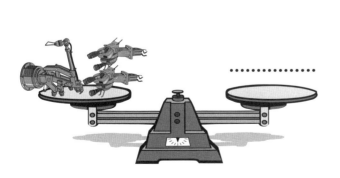

This is what equations are all about — balancing one side with the other. It's true — by working out the answers to these questions, you've done some equations already. Innit just great...

SECTION SIX — ALGEBRA

6.2   Questions on Powers and Roots

The little number at the top just means how many times you multiply the big number by itself — there's even a button on your calculator to do it for you...

Q1   Work out the square of these numbers:

a) 1 ....

b) 2 ....

c) 4 ....

d) 8 ....

Q2   What is the cube of these numbers?

a) 1 ....

b) 3 ....

c) 4 ....

d) 5 ....

Q3   Find the value of these:

a) 3^2 = ...

b) 5^2 = ...

c) 2^3 = ...

d) 6^3 = ...

e) 1^4 = ...

f) 2^5 = ...

Q4   Write these in index notation.

a) $2 \times 2 \times 2 \times 2$ = ...

b) $3 \times 3 \times 3 \times 3$ = ...

c) $6 \times 6 \times 6$ = ...

d) $5 \times 5 \times 5 \times 5 \times 5$ = ...

Q5   Calculate the following:

(Using the x^y button on your calculator)

a) 4^7 = ...

b) 5^6 = ...

c) 10^6 = ...

d) 2^{20} = ...

6.2   Questions on Powers and Roots

Q6   Work out the square root of these numbers:

a) 1 ....

b) 9 ....

c) 36 ....

d) 16 ....

Q7   Find the value of these:

a) $\sqrt{25}$ = ...

b) $\sqrt{4}$ = ...

c) $\sqrt{49}$ = ...

d) $\sqrt{64}$ = ...

Q8   Use your calculator to work out the following. Give your answers correct to 1 decimal place (to the nearest tenth).

a) $\sqrt{2}$ = ...

b) $\sqrt{10}$ = ...

c) $\sqrt{18}$ = ...

d) $\sqrt{24}$ = ...

e) $\sqrt{40}$ = ...

f) $\sqrt{50}$ = ...

g) $\sqrt{80}$ = ...

h) $\sqrt{40,000}$ = ...

Q9   If a square has an area of 144 cm², what is the length of one of its sides?

....

....

....

Square roots only look a bit tricky because of that funny symbol thing... but they're just the reverse of squaring, and you can do them on your calc anyway.

6.3 Questions on Number Patterns

Look at patterns in the numbers as well as in the pictures...
it'll be easier to work out what comes next.

Q1 Draw the next two pictures for each pattern.
How many matchsticks are used in each picture?

a)

....

b)

....

c)

....

d)

....

e)

....

6.3 Questions on Number Patterns

Q2 What are these sequences called, and what are their next 3 terms?

a) 2, 4, 6, 8, ..., ..., ...   Name = ...

b) 1, 3, 5, 7, ..., ..., ...   Name = ...

c) 1, 4, 9, 16, ..., ..., ...   Name = ...

d) 1, 8, 27, 64, ..., ..., ...   Name = ...

Q3 In the following number patterns, write down the next 3 terms:

a) 2, 5, 8, 11, ..., ..., ...

b) 7, 12, 17, 22, ..., ..., ...

c) 1, 11, 21, 31, ..., ..., ...

d) 49, 56, 63, 70, ..., ..., ...

Q4 Here are 3 sequences:

Sequence A	1, 4, 9, 16, 25,...
Sequence B	3, 6, 9, 12, 15,...
Sequence C	2, 5, 9, 14, 20,...

a) Write down the next three terms in sequence A.   ....., ..., ...

b) Write down the next three terms in sequence B.   ....., ..., ...

c) Explain how sequence C is obtained from sequences A and B.

....

....

....

OK, that last bit's quite tricky... look at the 1ˢᵗ term in A and B and find some different ways of getting the 1ˢᵗ term in C... then do the same for the 2ⁿᵈ, 3ʳᵈ, etc, until you find one that works for all of them.

6.4 Questions on Negative Numbers

*Negative numbers get a whole lot easier when you draw a number line...
because you can count along it to get your answers. Thermometer questions
are the most common in Exams, and they have the number line on anyway.*

Q1 Using the thermometer as a number line, work out
the temperature rise for each of the following:

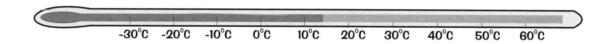

-30°C -20°C -10°C 0°C 10°C 20°C 30°C 40°C 50°C 60°C

a) 10°C to 40°C ....

b) -10°C to 0°C ....

c) -20°C to 30°C ....

d) -30°C to 40°C ....

e) -25°C to 5°C ....

f) -20°C to -15°C ....

Q2 Work out the drop in temperature for each of the following:

a) 30°C to -10°C ....

b) 20°C to -20°C ....

c) 0°C to -30°C ....

d) 40°C to -30°C ....

e) -10°C to -25°C ....

f) -5°C to -25°C ....

Q3 Arrange these numbers in order of size, smallest first.

3, 5, 0, -4, 245, 24, -9, 12.4, -34, -4

........., ..., ..., ..., ..., ..., ..., ..., ..., ...,

Q4 Find the value of each of the following:

a) 13–5 = ...

b) 6–7 = ...

c) 10–20 = ...

d) 4–11 = ...

e) -2+2 = ...

f) -10+5 = ...

6.4   *Questions on Negative Numbers*

Make sure you know the sign rules for multiplying and dividing negative numbers... even if you use your calc, it's a good way to check your answer.

Q5   **Work out the following:**

a) -4 × ¯3 = ...

b) 5 × ¯2 = ...

c) -12 ÷ ¯4 = ...

d) -8 ÷ 4 = ...

e) -20 ÷ ¯10 = ...

f) -4 × 4 = ...

g) 2 × ¯2 = ...

h) -36 ÷ ¯12 = ...

Q6   **What is the difference in height between the following points?**

a) H and T ....

b) R and H ....

c) W and R ....

d) W and T ....

e) H and W ....

f) T and R ....

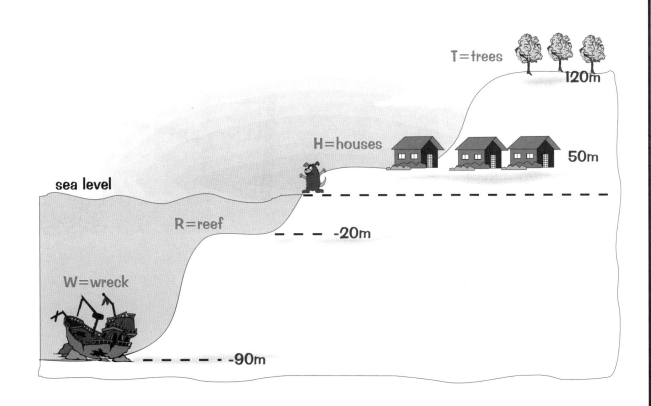

6.5   *Questions on Basic Algebra*

All you do is put all the things together that are the same...
in other words, you'd put 5x together with 2x and 4x, but not with 6y.

Q1   Complete the following, the first one is done for you:

a) ● + ● + ● + ● + ● = 5●

b) ● + ● + ● + ● = ...●

c) ✢ + ✢ + ✢ = ...✢

d) ☆ + ☆ + ☆ + ● + ● = ...☆ + ...●

e) ✢ + ✢ + ● + ● + ● + ☆ = ...✢ + ...● + ...☆

f) ☆ + ☆ + ☆ + ☆ + ☆ + ☆ + ✢ + ✢ + ✢ = ...☆ + ...✢

g) ✢ + ✢ + ✢ + ✢ − ✢ − ✢ = ...✢

h) ☆ + ☆ + ☆ + ☆ + ☆ + ● + ● − ☆ − ☆ − ● = ...☆ + ...●

Q2   Collect the like terms together.

a) $2x + 3x =$ ....

b) $5x - 4x =$ ....

c) $6x + 2y - 3x + y =$ ....

d) $10x + 3y + 2x - 3y =$ ....

e) $5x + 3y - 2z - 6y =$ ....

f) $-4z + 6x - 2y + 2z - 3y =$ ....

g) $15x - 4y + 3z - z - 11x + 5y - y - 4x + z =$ ....

6.5   *Questions on Basic Algebra*

Q3   Remember that x × x = x². Collect like terms:

a) y × y × y = ...

b) y × x = ...

c) x × 2x = ...

d) y × y + x × x × x = ...

e) p × p + 2q × q × q = ...

f) r × r × r + q² × q × 3p² = ...

Q4   Simplify by multiplying out the brackets.

a) 4(x + 3) = ...   d) 6(4x − y) = ...

b) 5(2x + 4) = ...   e) 2(5x − 3y) = ...

c) 3(3x + 1) = ...   f) p(2a + 3b) = ...

Q5   Multiply out the brackets and then collect like terms.

a) 3(x + 4) + 5(6x + 5)   = ... = ...

b) 4(3x + 3) + 2(2x − 7)   = ... = ...

c) 2(2x + 2) + 7(7x − 3)   = ... = ...

d) 3(5x − 5) + 6(8x + 8)   = ... = ...

e) 5(3x − 7) + 9(2x + 2)   = ... = ...

f) a(2b + 2) + a(5b − 6)   = ... = ...

<u>*Remember*</u> — *everything* <u>*outside*</u> *the brackets multiplies everything* <u>*inside*</u> *the brackets.*

6.6 Questions on Conversion Formulas

When you've got to find the number that went in, remember to work backwards from the output.

Q1 Work out the input/output from each of these number machines:

a)

? = ...

b)

? = ...

c)

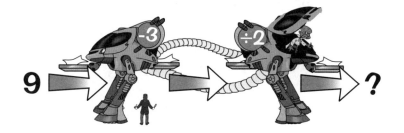

? = ...

d)

? = ...

Q2 Degrees Fahrenheit and Degrees Celsius are two different temperature scales.

$$F = \frac{9}{5}C + 32 \qquad C = \frac{5}{9}(F - 32)$$

a) Convert these temperatures from °C to °F:

i) 60°C ....

ii) 100°C ....

b) Convert these temperatures from °F to °C:

i) 41°F ....

ii) 77°F ....

6.7   Questions on Word Formulas

Q1   Frau Debus works out the weekly pocket money for each of her children. She uses the formula:

Pocket money (in pence) = Age in years × 20

Work out the pocket money for:

a) Karl, aged 10 years ....

b) Henri, aged 8 years ....

c) Ingrid, aged 5 years ....

Q2   To find P, multiply Q by two and then subtract four.

a) If Q has a value of 3, what is the value of P?

....

....

b) Write down a formula relating P and Q.

P = ...

c) Rearrange the formula so that Q is the subject.

....

....

Q = ...

d) If P has a value of 16, what is the value of Q?

....

....

Q3   Froggatt's hedgehog-flavoured potato crisps cost 50 pence a packet. Write down a formula for the total cost, T, of buying n packets of crisps.

T = ...

The trick is to split these into bits, or things'll get very confusing... write down each new scrap of information you read in Maths... then you'll have an equation.

6.8   *Questions on Trial & Improvement*

*Remember, find 2 <u>opposite cases</u>... one that's too big and one that's too small —
then just keep doing it 'till either you get the answer, or get near enough to it.*

Q1   Solve the equation $5x + 3 = 3x + 13$ by
the method of trial and improvement.

First estimate, $x =$ ....

Answer: $x =$ ....

Q2   Use the trial and improvement method to solve the quadratic
equation. Give your answer correct to one decimal place.

Solve $x^2 + x = 11$

Answer: $x =$ ....

MFW39